Wildly Successful

Is
Effective
Leadership
Obvious?

A Learning Fable
by Tracy Weber, Ph.D.

To Al

In December 2014, with the first draft of this book in the editing phase, a tragedy took place at Kaleidoscope Learning Center (KLC). KLC's first four-legged facilitator, Al (registered as "The Alchemist"), who is Carallot's salesman in this story, died very unexpectedly.

I can't explain the sadness I still feel in combination with heartfelt appreciation and love. When he walked upon the earth, "Schmalbert's" gifts to help humans were bountiful. His legacy will forever live on in all the lives he touched.

Table of Contents

Acknowledgements

Thank you first of all, to the horses, those from my past, those who are with me today, and the ones I look forward to loving in the future. You bring me insurmountable joy, are forever teaching me (I'm often a slow learner), offer me purpose, and bring meaning to my life.

This finished product is the result of a wonderful and supportive family, my daughters Carlye and Katie Hausbeck, a generous and caring future husband, Randy Bierlein, and my friend and niece, Shirley Wazny. Always in my corner are my sisters, Barb Luplow and Alice Sauve. Thank you "Weber Girls!" A shout-out to my former "family" of JL's Ranch & Saddlery, if it weren't for your love and guidance, I might never have become the person I am today. I'd also like to thank my parents, Ada and Arnie Weber. I hope that when you look down from heaven, you're smiling broadly at your crazy horse girl. Thank you for all those trips to JL's Ranch and for supporting (and sponsoring) me through riding lessons, horse shows, and all the trials and tribulations of a teen-aged barn-rat.

Without incredible opportunities to actually partner with horses and provide equine-assisted learning services, this story would not, could not exist (yes, that is very Dr. Seussian, so is the fable). There are too many two- and four-legged facilitators that I am grateful to have worked with to name. If you've ever "trusted the process" with me – my sincere gratitude and appreciation. Special recognition to Stacie Johnson, Amber Burkhardt-Sidebottom, and Sara Stants for your friendship, love, and willingness to read my drafts. Thanks also to Annie Rummel, Devora Demarco, Kevin Maize, Randy Ettema, Sylvia Dresser, and other members of the eight-pack that also includes Randy and me: Cheryl & Art Loeffler, Chip & Deb Sassone, Dave Johnston and Deb Hardin; I cherish your support and love.

Connie Larsen, artist and friend, brought this story to life through her incredible artwork. Connie, I am eternally grateful for your willingness to help with this project. Thank you for sharing this journey with me; it's been a fun excuse to reconnect. You are an AMAZING talent and an even more amazing human being!

My sincere appreciation to Emily Koenig and Stacey Trapani for their fabulous editing skills and, more importantly, for their continuous support and encouragement.

A shout-out to my Experiential Training and Development Alliance (ETDA) colleagues Faith Evans, Nate Folan, Melissa Churchard Hannon, Pam McPhee, Tony Richard, Marianne Skippa, and Paul Smith for helping direct the format of this book. Your advice and support came at a critical time, producing a future journey of collaboration for those who want to come along for the ride! Other significant colleagues that influenced this story are my esteemed friends at Next Element. Thank you Jamie Remsberg, Nate Regier, and Michele Ediger.

Lastly, a special thank you to a beautiful person and prolific outdoor travel writer Dixie Franklin. Back in my East Michigan Tourist Association days (circa 1990), when I first aspired to write a book, I met with Dixie and asked her about the process. Her profound words still hold great meaning for me, "Writers write." Dixie, I wish you were here on earth so I could see your smile because I'm FINALLY part of "The Authors Club." The first draft of this book was created in February of 2009 with the help of graphic artist Valerie Walderzak. The second "beginning" took place on April 2, 2013. The final "first draft" that led to this publication started on November 21, 2013. Writers write and writers who become authors persevere.

Introduction

As I write this introduction on a blustery February day in 2014, winds are gusting up to 34 miles per hour on the farm, the tempest (a fitting representative of this difficult winter) makes itself noisily and powerfully known. For Kaleidoscope Learning Circle's horses (who are the basis for the characters in this story), the wind is creating hay "tumble weeds" out of their breakfast, blowing them into my front yard, and away from their expectant mouths.

The wind, in addition to relocating a meal for the horses, has become a powerful spiritual messenger for me. Several years ago, I lived through a tornado (can you say, "really BIG winds") that awakened me to new possibilities and changed the course of my life. The tornado was a wake-up call from God/Spirit/A Higher Power that motivated me to start looking at my life choices. Not that my choices were "bad", it's more that they were out of balance. In a few short years after the tornado, I went from being a wife who did not have any horse contact, to choosing to be a divorced single parent embracing her passion for horses by creating a business, building a half-million dollar learning center, immersing herself in a life embedded in the equine-assisted learning (EAL) world, and embracing all parts of myself more fully – being instead of doing.

Today the wind spoke to me again, and even in its less perilous voice, there was a message. I found myself reflecting on the ice created in my side pasture. Upon further consideration, I realized the wind did not create the ice, the wind was only one of the necessary elements. In addition to the wind, to produce ice there must have been snow or at least water. In addition to the wind and snow, the temperature and humidity also had to be right for ice to form. And, in addition to the wind, snow, and temperature, the landscape also had to be open and exposed. I still (thankfully) have one pasture to put the horses in that did not become a literal skating rink overnight; which reinforces the premise that without ALL of the aforementioned conditions, ice does not just occur.

Right about now - you may be asking yourself, what in the world does ice formation have to do with introducing you to this book? Similar to the formation of ice, the creation of change, whether in organizations or individuals, requires several elements to come together, systemically, in the right way and under the right conditions. One goal of this story, Wildly Successful, is to introduce leveraging the positive attributes of relationship-centric AND task-centric leadership. The story seeks to help organizations shift from the time-consuming and often useless problem-solving technique of looking at "either/or" to a world of "and." "And" thinking helps us become more vulnerable and transparent, to bring the margins to the center, and to make decisions through a systemic lens. Tying back to the ice metaphor, one is best served by thinking systemically and leveraging the integration, intersection, and interdependence of two apparently conflicting leadership styles.

The story uses the example of company CEO Tigg shifting from a predominately task-oriented style of leadership to one that is more relational. Task-centric leadership is not inherently bad, nor is an entirely relation-centric leadership inherently good. I selected creating an unbalanced comparison of these two leadership approaches because of the growing body of evidence supporting the premise that the unbalance of being too task-centric is more common and the costs often invisible. When we learn to see opportunities through the lens of leveraging the positives of both relationship and task, the benefits increase the speed and sustainability of self and social change. For the Carralot Carrot Company (C3), the recognition of unintended consequences of the existing unbalanced task-heavy leadership style offers the opportunity to reframe their either/or problem-solving and decision-making process, creating new opportunities and yielding positive results.

In 350 B.C., Aristotle said that if communication is to change behavior, it must be grounded in the desires and interests of the receivers. In the more than 2000 years since then, this central idea remains largely unchanged. A design for change, then, is not a series of good ideas for how to do things better (which is what Tigg initially attempts), rather it is a series of steps that leads to something else. Once Tigg invites her management team, Al, Chuck, Phred, Diva, and Mick, to share their ideas without negative repercussions, C3 moves from an unhealthy to a healthy working environment. This movement demonstrates that organizations are transformed the moment people decide they are theirs to create.

I fell in love with David Hutchens fables (a model for this story) because of their humor, simplicity of story-telling, and the depth of information behind each foray into the worlds he creates, featuring lemmings, cave people, walruses, and a learning flock of sheep. David's gift is to strip away the pretense and show the underpinnings of failed decisions because of factors such as mental models, lack of dialogue, or the absence of a learning culture. Horses offer us similar opportunities for increased awareness, which is one reason equine-assisted learning (EAL) experiences can be powerfully life-changing. After reading David's books, it wasn't much of a stretch for me to envision Kaleidoscope's herd as the characters in a fable. Because of trademark and legal considerations, we have modified some of the barn names of our horses. If you're curious about their real names, visit www.myklc.com and click on "Our Approach" and about half-way down the page you will find our four-legged facilitators. It also wasn't a challenge for me to conceive the playful inside jokes and humorous names. As many friends who read the book in a draft stage told me, "It is so Tracy." At first I questioned whether that was "good" or "bad" then, following the example of Tigg, I reframed the message to, "It just is."

The big hairy idea (no pun intended this time) that pulled the story together was the role reversal of having a horse participate in a Human-Assisted Learning experience. Through this dynamic, I'm able to share how experientially partnering with horses helps humans identify underlying beliefs and overcome limiting ideas and assumptions. Horses genuinely respond with honest feedback reacting to the environment and energy. They create the opportunity for humans to recognize and understand what we are actually communicating, not what we "think" we are communicating. Horses see past any personal masks we wear, "live in the moment," and powerfully invite us to do the same.

The purpose of <u>Wildly Successful</u> is to educate, entertain, and evoke people to action. In addition to this book, we are developing a "living library" of programs, workshops, and learning resources to support the organizational and individual changes you seek. For opportunities to discover and explore ways to reframe relationships and create new possibilities please visit <u>www.wildlysuccessfulsolutions.com</u>.

Meet the Team at Carralot

Tigg, CEO

Tigg is committed to Carralot, and makes sure the values of the corporation are integrated throughout the organization.

Chuck, Carrot Processing Production Manager

Chuck makes sure the quality of the carrots being shipped to customers meet C3's high standards.

 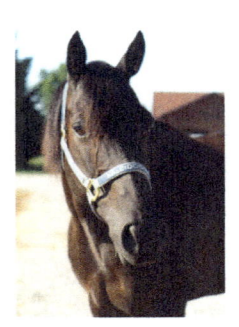

Diva, Accountant

Diva is logical, responsible and organized. She takes pride in her many awards, certificates, and plaques recognizing her accomplishments.

Carrot Corporation (C3)

Al, Sales Manager

Al is adaptable, charming and persuasive and wins C3 many accounts. He is resourceful, and full of life.

Phred, Human Resources Director

Phred is caring and compassionate, sensitive and warm. She has candles, pillows and soft music in her office; staff members feel comfortable there.

Mick, Field Manager

Mick oversees farm production. He likes his privacy and prefers to work in solitude. He's happiest when he is sitting on his tractor.

Chapter 1

Deeply Rooted in Task-Focused Leadership

Carralot Carrot Corporation (C3) is located in a beautiful region of Michigan, a rich agricultural area with many family farmers who have worked the same land for generations.

The town near Carralot is a typical farming community with a single gas station, local watering hole (literally), three churches, and, of course, a grain elevator. Farmers love "The Trough," a diner/drug store where they sit on rainy days drinking coffee, swapping stories, and sharing gossip.

Until recently, Carralot* had been wildly successful at growing, harvesting, and distributing carrots. The management team is comprised entirely of horses, all of whom are accomplished carrot farmers; they are also notable carrot eaters, and that's a different story.

At C3, knowledge is transmitted top down from leader to staff, communication is departmentalized, the past predicts the future,

---

*The company name is fitting because the management and staff "cared-a-lot" about their crops, and were "care-ful-not" to eat the profits.

attention is paid to risk containment, and the emphasis is where it should be – on external customers. Let's meet the remarkable management team:

Tigg is Carralot's CEO, meaning her decisions are final. Some might call her the "top dog" (in this case "top horse"). She is loyal and committed to Carralot, making sure the values of the company are integrated throughout the organization. She began working in the carrot industry when she was just a filly, fresh out of graduate school.

Chuck Brown is the Carrot Processing Production Manager, making sure the quality of the carrots being shipped to customers meets Carralot's high standards. He is spontaneous, creative, and playful. His energetic and animated personality helps keep the staff of the production department engaged in what can sometimes be mundane and tedious jobs.

Diva is the company's accountant. She is extremely logical, responsible, and organized. She takes pride in the fact that her workspace is ordered and efficient. One doesn't even have to ask her about her success, because she proudly displays the many awards, certificates, and plaques recognizing her accomplishments.

Al is the Sales Manager. He's a horse with real charisma, some might even call him a stud. His adaptable, charming, and persuasive personality serves him well, winning Carralot many accounts, most recently exports to Canada and Mexico. He is resourceful, self-sufficient, and full of zest and life.

Phred is a caring and compassionate Human Resources Director. She is sensitive, nurturing, and warm. Staff members at Carralot don't mind having to visit her in her office because it is such a cozy and comfortable place, with candles, pillows, and soft, soothing music.

Mick is the Field Manager, overseeing farm production. He has quite an imagination, is reflective, and calm. He likes his privacy, having his own space, and prefers to work alone in solitude. He's happiest when he's on his tractor, plowing the fields, letting ideas come to him, as if by magic.

On this day, the team finds itself a bit down. CEO Tigg has called Chuck, Al, Diva, and Phred into the conference room with hints of dire news.

"Team, take a look at our annual harvest reports," Tigg states, pointing to the reports hanging on the wall. They have never seen her so glum. "Our yields (this is a term used by farmers to indicate the number of carrots harvested, not a yellow sign designed to help motorists slow down), are down this year – way down. Any opinions or thoughts about what could be causing the decline?"

The management team (minus Mick, because even though he is part of the team he is considered just a field worker and doesn't get included in these important meetings) is shocked. They're doing what they've always done; how could this result in fewer carrots per acre, they collectively wonder?

Tigg suspects that there are things her Production and Sales managers aren't telling her; she just doesn't know how to get them to be more open. And, although Tigg is confident that Phred, head of human resources, is open with her communication and doing all she can to live up to the "caring" in the Carralot name, she sometimes thinks Phred can be a bit *too* caring. She hates to admit it, even to herself, there are times she finds Phred's perpetual sweetness and syrupy kindness more than a bit annoying. She decides that, because Diva is so logical and fact-oriented, she might be able to get the boys, Chuck and Al, to share. So when no-one answers

Any opinions about what could be causing the decline?"

her question about what they believe is causing the decline, she looks to Diva and gives her a subtle nod. Prior to the meeting, she authorized Diva to take a leadership role and ask a few questions of her fellow team members.

Diva, the bookkeeper, pipes up.

"Chuck, you're responsible for production, did you think to tell us that we were producing fewer carrots this year?

Chuck answers, somewhat sheepishly, "Nobody asked."

Next, she turns to Al.

"You're the head of sales. Did it ever occur to you to mention that you had fewer crates of carrots to sell?"

Chuck and Al are dumfounded. *Diva is the number cruncher, if anyone in the company would be aware of a yield reduction ahead of the annual report it would have been her...* they don't say anything though, as they are sure whatever they said would fall on deaf (though large and furry) ears.

Phred is near tears, she hates this feeling when there is dissention among her Carralot family. She wishes Mick were here in the management meeting; after all he's the Field Manager and might actually have some answers as to why the harvest was bad this year. Like Chuck and Al, though, she doesn't say anything. She remembers the last time that she spoke up with an opinion without being asked. It's too painful to be told, again: "That's not YOUR job."

Al, trying to be as charming as possible, clears his throat and summons the courage to ask the obvious question.

"Tigg, shouldn't *you* be telling us what happened last year and what to change moving forward? After all, you're the CEO." Chuck and the team are quick to agree.

A moment of awkward silence passes as the leaders of Carralot nervously look from one team member to the next.

Tigg seizes the moment and acts.

"I believe you're right!" she declares as she stands tall, pounding her hoof on the table. "The yields are ultimately my responsibility, quite frankly the success of the whole company depends on me. I don't know what I was thinking by asking Diva to get your input, it surely won't help C3 if we sit around having dialogue, we need action. I'll review our current policies, update them, and inform you of my plans at future management meetings. Meeting adjourned."

Mick, the Field Manager, who is outstanding in his field (well, technically he's not standing, he's sitting while driving the tractor) doesn't realize his life will soon change.

Yields have fluctuated in the past, and when they've been down, the field staff has carried an extra heavy load. Harder work. Longer hours for the same pay. Fewer resources and even less support. Poor Mick.

Mick, the Field Manager, who is outstanding in his field
(well, technically he's not standing, he's sitting while driving the tractor)
doesn't realize his life will soon change.

Chapter 2

You Can't Command Carrots (or Staff) to Grow

Later that week, Tigg meanders out to Mick's office to share a new policy change affecting him and his field crew.

"So Mick," Tigg says, "I want you to know how much we appreciate your hard work. You really are one of the big reasons our carrots are of such high quality and Carralot has such an excellent reputation."

"Gee, thanks, Tigg," Mick stammers. He's a bit skeptical about this unexpected visit from the CEO. He's aware that he only gets visits on this part of the farm when there is a problem. "I appreciate the compliments, though I really must get back to fertilizing. Is there something else you wanted?"

"Well, I'm afraid our annual production is down a bit from last year and there is going to be some girth-tightening. Sorry about that. You and your crew are going to have to step-it-up and help us out. I know we can count on you. Let's start by shortening the field crew's lunch hour down to 15 minutes. Surely, it's enough time to grab something to eat. That's all for now. You can get back to work," she states as she abruptly turns and heads back to her office.

Mick wilts. *Shorter lunch? Work harder? How will that improve our yields?* Mick wonders. *As usual, Tigg is quick to find a short-term solution instead of looking at the big picture. It occurs to me that this year's yield problem is a symptom of several aspects of the company that could use a shift, beginning with Tigg's task-centric leadership approach. If we had a better relationship, I would tell her. Not sure what I can do about it, though. Guess I better just get back to work, it's a good thing horses are such experts at fertilizing.*

The mood of the workers in the fields of Carralot is somber as crew members begrudgingly begin the first of many 15-minute lunch hours. Wait, isn't it now a lunch 'quarter-hour'?

Meanwhile, during a standard 60-minute lunch hour, the rest of the management team grumbles about its own problems. Phred shares her feelings with her peers.

"I feel so bad about the yields being down and am worried about what changes Tigg might make in order to get us back on track (horses aren't particularly fond of being "on the track" because they are usually the ones doing all the hard labor). As a management team, we attend the required weekly meetings, do what we are told AND," she laments, "We all do our jobs very well. Tigg has always led with a firm hoof, setting clear expectations and communicating by telling us what we need to know. As a company, we do all the right things too; we avoid risk, have a rigid pre-designed budget, and establish narrow organizational goals. Though, because Tigg has failed to anticipate trouble, we are the ones that are likely going to suffer the consequences. Maybe it's time we take matters into our own hooves."

Getting no support from her C3 teammates, she feels strongly enough to reach out to a respected colleague.

Phred leaves the lunch room to call her friend Bunny.

"Bunny, you're so happy at Easter Eggs Emporium (E3). You brag that it's a great place to work – even at the busiest time of year when you have to decorate and then hide thousands and thousands of eggs," Phred says. "How do you do it? What is your secret to success? We need help at Carralot Carrot Corporation and I'm hoping you have some ideas. What are you doing at E3 that we could be doing at C3?"

"Tell me more about what's going on, Phred. I want to help," Bunny replies.

"Production was down last year, which led to fewer sales and less income. Morale is lower than ever with everyone, except Tigg, feeling helpless. The management team is holding its breath waiting for the changes she is going to impose. What I can't put my hoof on is what I can do about the situation. We have the highest quality carrots anywhere, super field crews, and a talented, committed, management team. I'm afraid the problem might have something to do with our CEO, Tigg. Is that crazy?" asks Phred.

"Not crazy at all, Phred. Often, leaders with the best intentions are blind to the unintended consequences of their choices. Can you tell me more about Tigg's leadership style?" asks Bunny.

"Well, she is definitely the one in charge," Phred responds. "Tigg just doesn't seem to care enough to listen and be open to our feedback, or to be vulnerable and admit when she makes a mistake. She's the kind of leader who thinks she has all the answers, so she doesn't ask many questions. For example, Tigg says she wants our input, though it feels like she is just pretending to listen when we finally manage the courage to speak up. Honestly, it's like she has trained us to give her the answers she wants. That's no way to run a wildly successful company."

The more Phred reflects, the more she has to convey to Bunny.

"Then there's our Sales Manager, Al," she adds. "He's always off doing his 'sales thing.'" I think he's afraid to share with the management team any complaints from our customers about our products and services. Now that I think about it, he has tried a couple of times to discuss this at meetings and Tigg shut down his concerns, blaming the customers. She seems to have all of the answers."

"Also, we don't include Mick, the Field Manager, in our management meetings. His job is critical to our overall success, and unfortunately we don't treat him that way. I'd like to hear his insights. It's a missed opportunity that we never engage him or get his input."

Her thoughts turn next to the remaining member of the management team.

"And then we've got Diva – and boy is she one. To her, everything is data driven. She appears to be so unfeeling sometimes that it makes me want to cry. I agree it's important to pay attention to the numbers. Yet her focus is so very narrow, only looking out for our external customers and their past purchases. She doesn't even consider measuring areas of the company that are affected by other stakeholders or our internal customers."

"So you see, we have problems on many levels. I just don't know what to do." Phred sighs.

"Wow, that's a lot. From the outside, everything looks like it's running smoothly, though I know appearances are often deceiving," says Bunny.

"Well, our organization has looked pretty much the same since I've been here and, because we've been successful, for the most part, there hasn't been a reason to change," Phred says. "I'm tired of the way we operate. Communication is one-way and top-down. Information is departmentalized and the management team learns about key matters only on a need-to-know basis. We are solely data driven and our culture is competitive and individualistic.

"I almost hate to come to work in the morning," she confides. "Trouble is I need the paycheck, there are good benefits (we even get to take home the odd-shaped carrots), and I'm too comfortable to go out and look for something else. I feel like a seahorse in a pot filled with water who doesn't realize the water is slowly starting to boil. You know the old saying, the devil you know – in this case Tigg - is better than the devil you don't."

"It sounds as if Carralot is suffering from the unbalanced use of task-centric leadership." Bunny continues, "The positives of task-focused leadership is that it works well in a crisis situation, for example, because action cannot be delayed with discussion or debate. This 20th century leadership style was adopted because of the efficiency and expediency created by teaching people to obey directives. It seemed to work in all organizational settings because it appeared to reduce resistance to change. Though in reality, if one is too task-oriented without being relational as well, the leader can devalue individual creativity and internal motivation, causing people to act out of self-preservation and fear instead of internal motivation."

"Wow," responds Phred. "You sure know a lot about this stuff. Do you have a Ph.D. or something?"

"Thanks, no that's not it," Bunny answers. "Though you can call me Dr. Bunny if you like," she chuckles, recalling that her Uncle Bugs would ask what's up doc? whenever his friends entered a room.

"The reason I know so much about leadership styles is because E3 recently completed the best leadership training in our company's history. The training was conducted in a bit of an unconventional way – by experientially partnering with humans.* I can't say enough good things about it."

"Interesting ... tell me more," exclaims Phred.

"I'll start by explaining what I mean by experiential. In 1984, David Kolb defined 'learning and development' as the process of intentionally transferring knowledge from an experience. Human-Assisted Learning activities are based, in part, on his learning cycle, where participants have a concrete experience, reflect or debrief their observations, think about the concepts, and test those ideas through new experiences. A trained facilitator helps participants transfer the learning from the experience by making connections to choices in the real world. Make sense?"

"I think I understand, Bunny, though I'm not sure I get the part about the partnering with humans; what have they got to do with it?" Phred asks.

"When they are in a trusting place where they feel safe, humans have the capacity to respond authentically to the environment. In their organizations, who moves who has the power in relationships, and they are social creatures living and working in groups, teams, and families. Taken together, this means humans have the ability to offer honest feedback during experiential learning activities and

---

*Human-Assisted Learning with bunnies, horses, or other critters as participants/clients and humans as the experiential partner is a complete role reversal for Equine-Assisted Learning, where horses work with human participants/clients. Meaning, in the world of Carralot, the roles are switched between humans and non-humans. Clever, huh? Keep reading, it gets even better.

can help participants learn about their choices, assumptions, and underlying beliefs.*

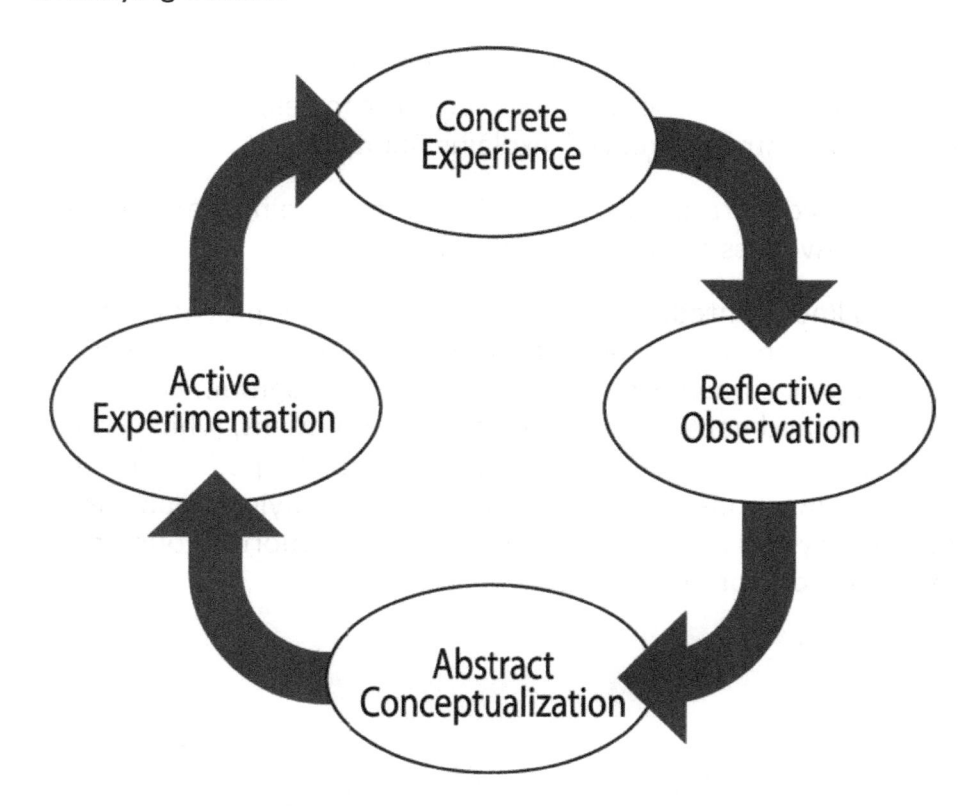

"The program E3 participated in was designed to help us improve our self-awareness and leadership skills. The facilitator told us they also offer other experiences focusing on topics such as team

---

*Note all the "qualifiers" in this sentence about working with the humans – with the right environment, humans respond authentically; though there are often limiting beliefs and blind spots that get in the way of sustainable and transformational change. With Equine-Assisted Learning (EAL), on the other hand, the horse partners DO actually provide honest, authentic feedback because they do not bring with them prejudices or hidden agendas. An additional caveat with horses is that equines are prey animals, meaning they are extremely sensitive to the environment, responding to the energy and intention of the humans, (who are predators, not prey) as well as other potential "horse-eating" things such as unfamiliar plastic bags or anything threatening. Equines provide authentic feedback based on the behavior of the human which, through dialogue and reflection, can lead humans to profound insight and self-discovery.

development, diversity, and innovation. Many times, they even create custom programs to address a specific need or for a particular group, such as women or youth. The first thing the facilitator did was meet with our CEO, Esther Rabbit, and asked her to define her desired learning outcomes. As you can tell, they use a very customer-centric approach," explains Bunny.

"That's so cool," responds Phred. "Thanks for helping me understand the effectiveness of human-assisted learning."

"As you know, Phred, the first step to any change process, whether personal or organizational, begins with awareness," Bunny explains. "During our human-assisted learning (HAL) program, we received authentic and genuine feedback from the humans, which created opportunities for new insight. Our facilitator helped the E3 team make connections to our relationships, identifying opportunities to make systemic organizational changes, supporting our desired long-term outcomes and behaviors."

Phred calls her friend Bunny who works at the Easter Egg Emporium, a very successful and wonderful place to work. Bunny says, "I'm glad you called because I might have just the right thing for Carrolot." "Interesting... tell me more!" exclaims Phred.

Bunny continues, "For example, we eliminated annual performance appraisals. We now use real-time feedback and dialogue. I mean, really, can you imagine giving your spouse or significant other an annual performance evaluation? Picture this. 'Hey, Honey Bunny, it's time we sit down and talk about the three areas where you excelled and one area you have room for improvement.' Really? It's amazing how organizations can get stuck doing what they have always done, so much so that they aren't aware that there are alternative ways of being.

"Experiential learning results are also longer lasting because the whole self is engaged, not just the mind," Bunny encourages. "The first thing I'd recommend is for Tigg to attend a demonstration. That way, she'll know if human assisted learning is the right fit for Carralot. The process is most effective with organizations and individuals that are open and curious; it's key that she tries it first to see if she is willing to be vulnerable."

Minnie
—
HR
Director

Chuck walks by Phred's office just as she hangs up the phone. He pokes his head in...

"Hey Phred, you look like you might have some good news for a change," Chuck observes.

"Well, actually Mr. Brown, I just might," she says. "I just got off the phone with my good friend, Bunny. She told me about an experiential leadership training E3 attended called human-assisted learning. Through partnering with humans, their management team learned about healthy relationships leading to increased productivity, improved morale, and lots of innovation. I think HAL would help us address some of our current challenges. Do you think Tigg would be willing to attend a demonstration?"

"Nah, I doubt it," responds Chuck. "Especially if it means taking us away from the office."

Phred mentions the Human-Assisted Learning Leadership training to Tigg. As Chuck predicted, Tigg isn't even willing to attend a demonstration. Tigg has been doing her own research on "sure ways" to improve C3; she's not interested in something as unconventional as working with humans.

Chapter 3

Human-Assisted Learning Helps Organizational "Eyesight" by Providing Insight

The planting season is just getting started when Chuck discovers an article in Carrot Topper (a trade publication ALL successful carrot farmers read) referring to Human-Assisted Learning. Without hesitation, he decides not to share it with anyone. After all, he knows from his conversation with Phred that Tigg already said "no" to the idea, so why waste everyone's time.

Locals assemble at the Trough Restaurant on a random Friday for evening refreshments. As usual, after reliving each play of last night's high school football game where the Eagles (literally) flew to victory, the conversation turns to work.

"I'm just curious," asks Al. "Does anyone have any leadership training secrets they are willing to tell me about? We're facing some challenges right now at C3 and I'd like to be able to contribute."

"Well," answers Barney Owl, "At Roosters Rockin' Realty, our leadership team begins each project by creating a shared vision.

In this issue...

"Getting to the ROOT of leadership challenges through Human-Assisted Learning" by Pea Pole and Hugh Mann
Page 3

"When you have too many critters on the farm, you quit singing" by renowned author E.I. McDonald
(also known as "old" McDonald to his friends)
Page 6

"Purple Carrots-the Newest Trend" by Barney Dinosaur
Page 8

"Talking things out, the key to effective communication" by Mr. Ed
Page 9

Do you know what a shared vision is?"

"Of course I do," responds Al. "It's where everyone is on the same page – right?"

"Shared vision goes beyond just assuming everyone is on the same page. A shared vision integrates each individual's personal vision, producing a shared picture of the future they collectively desire. Developing a shared vision encourages curiosity and inquiry because participants seek to accurately understand each other's beliefs," responds Barney. "Creating a shared vision is a process that invites healthy conflict, rich dialogue, and celebrates diversity of ideas. Preferably, your organizational culture supports the exploration of a shared vision as a continuous dialogue, not just a statement that is printed on business cards and etched into a plaque on the boardroom wall. The process of creating a shared vision brings all the voices into the room, mobilizing all employees to action, and connecting each individual to the bigger picture."

"Oh, I get it," says Al, still not entirely sure he does.

The following week, Diva, Al, Chuck, and Phred (still sans Mick) gather for the required weekly management meeting. The conversation centers on their current challenges.

"I know," suggests Diva. "Let's try taking some of these well-known personality tests. There is one I heard of that uses color to help you understand personality differences. For example, you might be labeled a buckskin, paint, or bay. Somehow, labeling an individual by a certain color helps you understand yourself and manage others... " Diva trails off.

"Nah, those don't work," says Al. "I've taken several personality assessments like that as part of my sales training. I learned different things matter to different individuals based on their profile. Big whoop. Already knew that just from working together. What I didn't learn by just taking those self-assessments was how to leverage that knowledge into something that helps build meaningful, healthy, authentic relationships."

Chuck jumps in, "Maybe we should all read the same leadership book, then get together and talk about it. I heard two great ones are: <u>Leading without a Rope and Halter</u> by Whin Hee or <u>Spurred on to New Leadership Challenges</u> by Nick Er."

"Thanks for the suggestion Chuck. I just don't feel that would work here," responds Phred despondently. "In my experience, collectively reading a book, no matter how great, won't necessarily lead to a sustainable positive impact. For change to happen and learning to take place, the individuals must commit to something more, possibly a workshop or use other training tools. It also helps if there is a culture of openness, trust, and vulnerability and we sure don't have that here... at least not yet."

"Yeah," admits Chuck, "That's for sure."

Tigg enters the room, just in time to hear the management team come up empty on ideas or solutions. *Figures. That's why she leads this company.* Their lack of creativity and engagement reaffirms her commitment to using a firmer hoof, because clearly that is what it's going to take to make positive change happen.

There is a well-known management motivational metaphor involving a carrot and a stick: where the carrot is a reward or positive incentive  and a stick – um – isn't. Tigg is a firm believer in this philosophy. In that moment, the CEO of Carralot decides that it will serve C3 if she is more deliberate and intentional about incentivizing good behavior and punishing employees when they stray from her directives. She plans to do this through secretly keeping track of how each of her managers respond to her new initiatives, then she can use the information to hold each of them accountable.

Her realization about the critical importance of monitoring the management team gives Tigg even more confidence about the new policies she's about to share with them. She excitedly explains to the team that she diligently revisited C3's organizational goals and, after thorough review, she concluded that they have some amazing opportunities and all they need to do is make a few minimal changes. They'll begin by getting more production out of the field workers through instituting a 15-minute lunch hour for the field staff. She reports that she has already put this policy into place by talking with Mick, and she's expecting that the management team will immediately celebrate her and recognize her dedication. For some reason though, they all seem almost disappointed. Curious. *No matter*, she thinks to herself, *wait 'til they hear the rest...*

She continues by telling them that she's also decided that Carralot's external customers deserve more attention and resources, meaning that starting today there will be a freeze on all staff training and professional development (except for her, of course, because she's the CEO). The team responds by physically slumping down in the chairs just a bit lower. Tigg doesn't notice, she's too eager to share her next idea.

Last but not least, she explains, the program she believes will really energize Al, is that C3 is going to implement a new sales contest in order to get salespeople working more like a team; the competition is sure to be fierce and she is personally excited to see who wins.

Al looks questioningly at Tigg. *Is she out of her flipping mind?* he thinks to himself. *The contest she is describing will undermine the existing payment structure at C3 and is certain to disrupt what is currently one part of the organization that is working well. Besides that,* he muses, *wouldn't it have made sense to include him in the conversation about a sales contest?*

Tigg is too busy mentally patting herself on the back to notice Al's reaction to her "great idea." She almost can't believe her own brilliance. Typical for Tigg's leadership style, she plows through with her agenda, ignoring the obvious signs that the team is not engaged or in alignment. Tigg does not seek to understand her team members' concerns, nor does she make any attempt to gain support. She does make sure, though, that everyone knows her opinion and the required expectations. These new policies will work, there's no doubt about it. Or is there?...

After the meeting, Tigg is back in her office reflecting on her genius when she is suddenly struck by the management team's less than enthusiastic response to her new policy initiatives. It occurs to her that she did ALL the talking. There weren't any comments. Not a single question and nobody sought clarification. Why didn't her ideas energize the team? It's a mystery to her.

She decides that instead of focusing on the team's lack of enthusiasm for the new policies, she'll just have to find other ways to incentivize and motivate them.

She remembers when she worked at the Caring Carrot Company, they supported their team members by decorating walls with motivational posters featuring beautiful pictures and catchy, (supposedly) meaningful sayings. She thinks to herself, maybe that will work; it can't hurt. A horse is a horse, of course, of course, and a meaningful SLOGAN is so much more! She goes online and buys a horse trailer load of motivational posters, plaques, and coffee mugs. This, she thinks to herself, will work.

It doesn't.

When the motivational knick-knacks don't help the Carralot team authentically communicate and simply end up decorating blank ugly walls, Tigg decides to incentivize the team with a company-wide contest. That, she concludes, will make them WANT to work harder and then C3 will surely get prosperous results. She researches the very, very, very best incentive programs, connecting with several "experts" who claim they can change the C3 culture, fixing her obvious employee motivation problems.

Tigg decides to implement what she calls the "smile campaign." Through her research, one constant is that happy people are more productive. Smiles correlate to happiness, happiness correlates to productivity. Perfect.

She unwaveringly implements a sure-win program (in her mind). For the contest, smiles earn points. The more smiles, the more points; the more points, the more chances employees have to win. There are prizes of trips to exotic destinations such as Pony Paradise Island and happy bucks to purchase bushels of apples and peppermint treats. She directs hourly staff to decorate anything that is not moving or breathing with balloons, banners, and smile stickers. There is even a daily winner of a scratch-off smile card

for bonus points. Even though the "smiles" at C3 look at lot more like grimaces of pain, Tigg is sure this will work...

It doesn't.

Feeling weary that all her initiatives are failing to improve morale, she resolves to ask a friend for advice. At her weekly Rotational* meeting, Tigg talks with her friend Charlene Spider. Charlene is the CEO of Webb's Wonderful Weavers (W3).

---

*Rotational is a member-based service club that brings together community business leaders weekly for food and fellowship. The members volunteer for service projects and events, raising money to help eradicate diseases, provide clean water, and support a variety of other causes.

"Hey Char," asks Tigg, "Would you be willing to share your honest opinions about your leadership culture at W3?"

"Sure, Tigg, happy to share," responds Charlene. "We're committed to balancing relationship and task through creating a culture that invites healthy conflict, is open, and resourceful. We encourage dialogue and focus on asking the right questions, not simply trying to find the best answer. Does that help?"

"Sort of...I guess," answers Tigg hesitantly.

Tigg doesn't really know what Charlene is talking about and does not want to appear stupid in front of her friend. Open? Resourceful? Tigg is all that and more, she thinks to herself. Isn't that the foundation of any good leader, she muses. Ironically, if she only asked Charlene a few questions, she would show her vulnerability, modeling exactly the concept her friend referenced. Unfortunately for Carralot, that is not what happens.

Tigg makes one last failed attempt at facilitating a paradigm shift within Carralot. Her final hope to get the company back on track, improve morale, and raise yields is by requiring everyone on the management team to read the same leadership book. Once they've read it, she will tell them the important lessons she's identified in the book and how they are going to implement them at C3. She graciously (in her opinion, especially since she had earlier decided to cut training funding) gives each of them copies of <u>Leading Your Team to Water and Making Them Drink</u> by Have U. Herd. This book has made all the important top seller lists and is touted in the Carrot Topper as THE BEST leadership book currently on the market. This will do the trick for sure, she thinks to herself.

Reading the book doesn't help Carralot. No surprise (to us – right?)

In spite of her failed attempts at fixing the Carralot staff, Tigg enjoys a moment of self-appreciation for all the effort and hard work she has done. She is confident that she has tried everything cutting edge and diligently researched other successful approaches. The good news for all involved, Tigg thinks to herself, is that she is attending a leadership conference this weekend. If nothing else, she reflects, she'll get a chance to reconnect with friends, laugh at retelling the same old jokes, and create a few new memories. She only wishes the conference were being held in Greener Pastures, Florida instead of Wagon Pullers, Wisconsin. She sighs to herself, appreciating the freedom of a name like Greener Pastures and wishing Carralot were currently grazing there.

Chapter 4

The Worm (and the Carrot) Turns

Back on the farm in the lunchroom ...

"I'm getting tired of all this motivational baloney that Tigg keeps tossing at us," Chuck tells the group.

Al agrees. "I know what you mean. Yet, what can we do? When our CEO has a plan, there's no changing her mind."

"I really enjoyed reading <u>Leading Your Team to Water and Making Them Drink</u>," Phred shares. "I built myself a cozy fire, turned on some soft background music, and all was well with the world. That is, until I got to the part about 'making them drink' - brutal. I'm not comfortable MAKING anyone do anything. Like my father used to say, 'I'm a lover, not a fighter.'" She chuckles, remembering that her dad said that whenever he was trying to avoid an argument.

While Phred and the boys are having their conversation over carrot soup, Diva is furiously crunching numbers in her office. She's convinced that there must be a logical way to help Carralot. "I'll keep working even harder and surely I'll find a way to help the team," she tells herself.

Tigg's experience at the Leadership Conference begins just as she imagined. She has a great time hee-hawing with Don Key and jawing with Whitey Shark. They reminisce about last year's conference and how they learned so much from the keynote speaker, Hilar I. Tea, whose powerful message was about the health benefits of laughter.

After a lovely buffet breakfast, including her favorite alfalfa and sugar cube biscuits, Tigg asks Dorene Duck, Dougy Duck, and Greta Goose what morning break-out sessions they plan to attend.

"Gee, I don't know," respond Duck, Duck, and Goose almost in unison.

"All of the sessions seem to have merit," says Greta. "Though, you know, I think the most interesting is this one about Human-Assisted Learning (HAL). As a business leader, it's more transferable and relevant for me than the ones on healthcare or taxes. I hire people that are experts on those topics. The conference e-book describes the HAL session as experiential, meaning the session won't be a 'sit and git' or 'sage from the stage.' I much prefer learning something where the session builds on what I already know, is purposeful, and respects me as a participant. What do you guys think?"

"That makes sense to me...and it might just hold the answers to the challenges I'm having at Carralot lately," Tigg says. "I recall one of my employees, though I can't remember who, mentioning something about this HAL concept. Even if it isn't that great, at the very least we'll be moving around and that's a good thing after such a hearty breakfast – love those apple fritters!"

Dougy chimes in, "Well, our company is too small to have an expert in this new healthcare stuff and it is so confusing... I'm headed to that one."

"I'm lucky," responds Dorene. "My administrative assistant handles all the healthcare and tax stuff, so I'm open to trying something new and, like you said Tigg, it would be good to flap my wings a bit. Let's go to the Human-Assisted Learning session!"

Tigg, Dorene, and Greta arrive at an indoor arena, where the Human Assisted Learning break-out session is taking place. There's a circle of chairs for the participants, a flipchart, and a facilitator chatting with other conference attendees. In an enclosed designated area, near the circle of chairs, there are six humans of different sizes and colors wandering around seeming to get comfortable in their surroundings.

The facilitator welcomes everyone and introduces herself. She explains that the HAL delivery model her company, Kaleidoscope's Klever Konsultants (K3) prefers is two co-facilitators. In addition to her, she will work with a partner who is trained as a Human-Assisted Learning Specialist.

"Our HAL Specialist today is Mojo Mutt," she announces.

Mojo waves his paw and smiles broadly. As we know, dogs are "man's best friend" and fortunately for this group Mojo is a life-long human lover. He's studied humans since he was a pup. Cats are also known for being effective HAL specialists, though they have the reputation as being a bit too "God-like" and not as loyal or eager-to-please as dogs.

The facilitator picks up where she left off...

"The reason K3 believes in having two facilitators for a group is, number one, to help support the physical and emotional safety of both the participants and humans. The other advantage to having more than one facilitator is that each brings their own unique point of view, which can provide different perspectives and help clients' learning," She explains.

Mojo recognizes his cue and begins the human safety talk.

"Before we begin our first activity, I'd like to ask if anyone has any concerns about going into the pen with the humans. Because you will be working with live animals, part of our job is to set you up for success and help you learn some ways to take responsibility for your safety."

"Do the humans bite and kick?" asks Doubting Thomas Turtle.

"Yes, they can bite and kick," responds Mojo, "and what's relevant is to learn more about when they are likely to do either and what the risks are for you. Let me expand on that. Humans are predators, so when they feel threaten they will do what they can to protect themselves. Fortunately, they typically offer us warning signs before they take any action. Another thing to keep in mind, is that humans work in a hierarchy, so 'who moves who' gives participants' information about the order of the leadership. Lastly, we have a rule that you don't want to put anything in a human's mouth that you want to keep, because behind those soft lips are some sharp teeth. The best thing you can do is to stay calm and present in the moment. Does anyone have any other concerns?"

Tigg muses to herself, *I sure wish the humans had ears and tails like horses do, ones that show our emotions.* Pinned ears and a rapidly swishing tail indicates an un-happy or frustrated equine, meaning it's time to pay attention and be wary of what could happen next!

The facilitator explains that she'll be asking for just eight participants to serve as members of the volunteer clump. (We could use the word "group" and clump is so much more fun!) The rest of the group, as active observers, will still have the opportunity to learn something about themselves and others, even though they will not be actively participating in the experiences with the humans.

"Everyone who is open and reflective may find personal insights," she explains, "Because the HAL process offers the chance to explore your decisions, assumptions, and beliefs. The debriefing process, held after each activity is finished, is designed for everyone to make connections between the experiential activity and choices in everyday life. One of today's goals is to look for patterns of behavior that may be getting in your way of effectively communicating with others. The group will also identify successful behaviors, a positive psychology approach, and how to support creating even more of the future we desire."

After a brief explanation of Human-Assisted Learning's history, including an explanation of why this learning process can be so effective,* the facilitator asks for eight volunteers to participate

---

*We briefly introduced experiential learning and HAL in Chapter 2 through the conversation between Minnie and Bunny. Remember, the true-to-life scenario is a description of equine behavior (not human). Some of the key reasons Equine-Assisted Learning (EAL) is effective is because equines live in a herd, are prey animals, have a hierarchy, provide authentic feedback, and so on.

in two activities with the humans. She explains that the humans will be at liberty and able to wander in a designated area, allowing them the freedom to make choices either to leave the clump or engage with the volunteers.

Tigg, Dorene and Greta look at each other and shrug, almost as if to say, "We might as well volunteer – we are here to learn, after all – right?"

Before the participant volunteers engage with the humans, the facilitator distributes 3x5 cards and pencils to the active observers, explaining that it is their job to identify two different types of behaviors they notice during the first activities. They are asked to note when they witness effective and ineffective actions by the volunteers, as well as examples of ineffective behavior from the volunteers. She reassures them that there are no right or wrong answers, that by capturing their observations in writing, they will support the goal of increased self-awareness.

The volunteer participants are invited to begin with an activity called "Meet and Greet." This is where the participants enter the designated area and "meet" each of the humans, in any manner they deem appropriate. The facilitator invites the clump to do this without talking, since research shows that most of our communication is non-verbal and by eliminating talking we become more present in the moment. "Once all eight of you have introduced yourself to each of the humans, please come over and rejoin the larger group," she concludes.

After the participants complete the "meet and greet" activity with the humans and join the larger group, the facilitator begins the debriefing session.

"Tell me what struck you about that experience," she asks.

"Well," says Doubting Thomas Turtle, "Nobody liked me."

"What makes you say that?" the facilitator inquires.

"Weren't you watching? They all had their heads down, some walked away, and the rest just stood there," he responds.

"That's not what I saw," Windsong Cardinal chimes in. "Actually, it looked to me like you were the one that wasn't interested."

The facilitator, seeking open dialogue and not wanting unhealthy conflict to develop, intervenes.

"You both saw the same interaction behavior, Thomas not engaging with the humans, and yet you each interpreted it differently. Can we agree that the facts of the behavior interaction are identical?" She asks. The participants nod in agreement. "What led to the different conclusions, then," she continues, "is your belief systems about the meaning behind the behavior. Misinterpreting other's actions can lead to all sorts of communication challenges, which is why it is so important to stay curious. Thomas and Windsong, thank you both for the courage to share your thoughts so quickly."

Opal Opossum enthusiastically pipes up, "I thought that if I played dead, the humans would ignore me... and they didn't. They were inquisitive and came over to see what I was doing. It reminded me that when I play dead at other times, I'm the one that loses out on the relationship, not the other way around. Thanks so much for this experience."

The debriefing lasts about 20 minutes, with the participants and observers sharing their insights, asking questions, and making connections. Because this is an introductory demonstration and not a full, customized program, the facilitator is sensitive to the time constraints and keeps the program moving to stay on the conference schedule.

"The next thing we will ask our volunteers to do," she explains, "is to work together and guide the humans through a pre-determined path without touching them or using any outside resources. This activity allows us an opportunity to explore the balance between relationship and task. During "meet and greet," the volunteers simply asked the humans to be humans, meaning they had the choice to walk away or disengage – and some did, right Thomas?" He smiles. "That exchange was all about relationship because there was not a specific task involved. Now, they are going to ask the humans to do something or, in other words, give them a task. We often have to invite others to do something that is not their idea or something they may not want to do. Effective leaders are able to motivate others in ways that make what they want done easy and what they don't want difficult. They have the ability to take an "and" approach rather than "either task or relationship." Any questions?"

"From where I waddle," quacks Doreene, "Tigg and Cardinal created more chaos than effective leadership."

There aren't any actual questions, just a few confused looks and lots of movement. Windsong starts aggressively chirping about who should do what. Opossum is off in his own little world, and the rest of the group moves around aimlessly; except for Greta, Dorene, and Tigg who work together to try to get the human closest to them through the path. When standing in front of the humans and clapping doesn't work and the human walks away, the real chaos starts. The humans are going every which way. It's clear they have no idea what is being asked of them. That's when Tigg loses it.

Tigg finds herself shouting, telling the volunteer participants their roles, where they should stand, what they each should be doing. She even instructs the active observers to get involved, yelling at them to wave their arms (or fins or legs, as the case may be) in the proper direction.

What a bunch of idiots, she thinks to herself. I *mean, really, this is so obvious. By getting all the energy moving in the same direction, the humans will have clear communication and the task will be easy, just like the facilitator explained would happen with effective leadership. If they would just listen to me... yet they don't.* (Sound familiar?)

After what feels like days, though it is only 45 minutes, the facilitator calls the group of volunteers together and asks them to share their thoughts, feelings, and opinions.

"What struck you about this experience?" she begins.

Tigg eagerly starts, "I tried taking a leadership role and unfortunately no one would listen. I don't understand why no one got on board. I had a good plan. If everyone would have just done what I told them, we could have gotten the humans through that path five or six times, maybe more."

"Actually," points out Windsong, "I, too, was trying to take a leadership role and quite frankly, my plan was better than yours. It's just that you are bigger and louder than I am."

"From where I waddle," quacks Dorene, "you two created more chaos than effective leadership. The humans mirrored our confusion by roaming around and not engaging with anyone. I don't blame them for not going through the path; we sent them lots of mixed messages. Besides, going through a path was our goal not theirs."

"I agree," Greta Goose jumps in. "We could have been successful if we had a shared vision and focused on one human at a time. Kind of like flying in a 'V' formation with a clear leader."

The facilitator, who purposefully gave the participants the time to share their thoughts and opinions, now speaks up,

"So, did it really matter if you got a human through the path?" she asks.

The volunteer clump, looking more frustrated than ever, responds either by vigorously nodding "yes" or by asserting, "Of course, you told us that was the goal of the activity."

"You may remember I explained that this activity allows us to explore the balance between relationship and task." The facilitator continued, "The task was defined as getting humans through a path, the actual goal of the activity, and the entire break-out session, is to offer you the opportunity to increase your self-awareness. Meaning, my definition of success was creating an environment or opportunity for you to learn. And did you?"

"You mean it didn't matter if they got a human through the path?" verifies one of the active observers.

The facilitator nods affirmatively and gently smiles.

A ripple of understanding runs through the arena. One can almost see the "light bulbs" coming on for the participants as they experience new insights and "aha" moments. They all learned something about themselves during the activity.

"Each moment of our lives, we make choices about our actions and responses. Much of the time, we are in a habitual mode, even with our emotions. Our brains are wired with two ways to perceive the world, one is by default and the other direct. Ask yourself how you showed up in this experience; were you mindful of your choices and the meaning behind them? Did you actively listen to one another's ideas or were you just waiting for your turn to talk?"

She continues, "HAL is a perfect practice field for increased self-awareness. Through becoming more aware, we can then make conscious choices to intentionally eliminate behaviors that are  ineffective and replicate those that are effective. One of the keys to becoming wildly successful is to focus on process, or the 'how' you are doing something, not content or the 'what' you are doing."

At the close of the session, the facilitator tells the group about exciting new research providing evidence that Human-Assisted Learning enhances emotional intelligence, improves life skills, and supports positive outcomes for organizations and individuals. In fact, she goes on, there are colleges and universities around the world that offer credit-bearing courses and degrees in both HAL and Human-Assisted Mental Health. Before thanking the participants and releasing them for lunch, she wraps up by explaining that, "When partnering with humans for either personal growth or professional development, the expertise of the facilitators is significant. It's not just about the human or the experience. The process is most effective when there are expert "interpreters" who support participants in making connections between the HAL experiences to other life choices. This is where lasting and transformational change begins. HAL is a cutting-edge process poised to change the way the world delivers education and mental health services."

Chapter 5

Carralot Cares a Lot for Leveraging Collective Leadership

Tigg is deeply reflective as she walks to lunch. She's mindful that, during the Human-Assisted Learning experience, she responded like she normally would at Carralot, taking charge and telling others what to do. Yet, that didn't help the volunteer clump get a human through the path. She has an "aha" moment, when it occurs to her that maybe her leadership approach could be the root cause of the recent

challenges at Carralot. She recalls how disengaged and morose her management team has been lately, even though they are doing all that she is telling them to do.

Fortunately (and not accidently, by the way), Tigg selects an afternoon breakout session focused on leadership and moving your organization from its existing state to a desired way of being. To her, the opportunity to attend this break-out session on the heels of the HAL session feels like some form of divine intervention (Duh? Actually, it's the main point of this story).

The presenter, Seanan Giraffe, welcomes them and begins by explaining that there are thousands, if not millions, of leadership theories. He promises that he won't bore the group by introducing them to ALL of them, he says with a rather throaty chuckle. Instead he is going to introduce the concept enhancing leadership through leveraging both relationship-centric and task-centric styles. Then, he is going to walk the group through two activities designed to help them recognize their style and possible alternatives.

After clearing his long giraffe throat, he explains that, "When an organization or group of people are facing challenges, one option is to leverage the positive aspects of both relational and task leadership. If you lean too much toward one style and are unbalanced, you'll have negative consequences. For example, if you recognize a desire to grow in the relational side, you'll find that more collaborating increases buy-in and a sense of shared ownership by everyone because each individual is engaged and part of the decision-making. Through the open process of dialogue and healthy conflict, participants build trust. The trust combined with individual empowerment helps build a new generation of leaders, who in turn are more willing to tackle tough issues and find new ways of solving problems which leads to substantive and sustainable results."

"On the other hand," Seanan continues, "if you find that you are focusing too much on a relational style, you lose the effectiveness of a clear chain of command, decisions take longer, and the boundaries between personal and professional relationships may be cloudy. The key is to identify ways to identify, grow, and support the positive aspects of BOTH leadership approaches. This is an 'and' not an 'either/or' way of looking at the world. You also want to think systemically, across the entire organization, seeking to create long-term, sustainable, results."

Seanan then distributes a form, inviting participants to identify their existing leadership styles. Tigg takes a deep breath, as she's already sensing this experiment will result in an uncomfortable look at herself. Then, before she begins writing, she reminds herself: "Self," she says, "one of the first steps to change is awareness." She digs in and creates something that she recognizes as her - she is leaning too far toward a task-centric approach.

Next, the facilitator, while distributing a second form, invites participants to compare and contrast their existing state with their desired state of being.

Tigg looks sadly at her paper describing the existing state. She is thankful that she decided to be honest with what is going on at Carralot, even though it is difficult to admit. In that moment, she decides that her desired state is pretty much the opposite of what she is doing now. Newly motivated, she gets to work writing out her desired state.

Once everyone stops writing, the presenter puts table-top signs out on eight round tables, one representing eight areas of interest: Leadership, Knowledge Structure, Communication, Learning, Success, Risk-Taking, Goal-Setting, and Organizational Culture. He asks the participants to select one area where they want to start moving from an existing state to the desired state. While everyone is gathering their stuff, he reminds them that for a healthy discussion, each participant is best served when everyone is curious, and they can support that by asking questions such as "tell me more" or "where else does this show up in your life?" He also encourages the participants to not hijack the conversation, by saying something like "I know what you mean" and then talking about themselves. If they actively listen to each other and allow the conversation to go wherever it is intended, they may be surprised what they learn.

Finally, before releasing them to find their tables, he shares the following questions as possible conversation starters.

1. What is the crossroads on which you find yourself in this area of your business?

2. How committed are you to facilitating a change from existing to desired?

3. How resourceful, open, and persistent do you plan to be while transitioning from the existing state to the desired state?

4. To what extent are you willing to invest in the well-being of the whole?

The participants engage in active small group conversation for 40 minutes. The energy in the room is palpable and Seanan has a difficult time re-convening them when it's time to come back together for a large group discussion. He then leads a brief discussion about what they discovered during their conversations. The take-aways include learning they had more similarities than

differences, they were not alone in some of the challenges they face, that there are often unintended consequences creating barriers to change, and the ambiguous nature of Seanan's questions created a rich and powerful dialogue for each of them.

Following the session, Tigg feels compelled to thank Seanan for his wisdom. She is so excited about the possibilities! She can hardly wait to get back to Carralot...her brain is working in overdrive with ideas. She starts writing them down, so she doesn't forget (she's a horse, after all, not an elephant!):

*Start with self. Be transparent and own your mistakes. Ask employees to trust her and help her as they explore and practice a new way of being (not just doing).

- Redefine our success based on relationships, not just numbers. Get everyone involved in deciding what matters at Carralot and collectively decide how best to assess when the company is moving in a positive direction.

- Invite Mick to the management meetings and give the field staff back their 60-minute lunch hour. Oh my, what was I thinking when I made that decision, she wonders to herself?

- Call Charlene and tell her about Human-Assisted Learning. She's sure to love it and it's a great fit for W3. Heck, it's a great fit for every leader who is willing to subordinate their ego.

Once back at Carralot, Tigg brings the team together for the regular weekly management meeting.

"I'm so excited to share the things I learned at the conference," Tigg begins.

The management team, including Mick (who is looking perplexed and wondering why he was invited and what he did wrong), are distracted, looking out the window or at their phones, not really paying attention as they've heard all this before (or so they think). They did notice that the usual boring agenda wasn't sent out in advance and isn't on the board table. Hmmm.

"I can see you're expecting the same old, same old," Tigg continues. "Well, think again! First thing we're going to do instead of our usual department check-in is to spend a little time playing a game."

All heads look up and they start paying attention. Well, this is different, they think.

"A...game?" stutters Diva. She isn't really into game-playing, unless it involves logic or numbers and she is guessing that's unlikely, judging by Tigg's enthusiasm.

"Yes, a game," responds Tigg. "This game, well actually it is an assessment, will help us look at eight key areas within Carralot to see if there is room for improvement."

Tigg already knows there is room for improvement. She introduced the assessment that way to see the reaction of the management team and they don't disappoint. They look at each other in surprise and astonishment. Did they hear her correctly?

"Room for improvement?" inquires Phred. "I'm not sure what you mean?" Phred is a little whip-shy with Tigg because in the past, when she has shared the way she feels, she's walked away feeling hurt and disappointed.

"Yes, room for improvement. I know there is a lot of it, so that isn't really the question," Tigg continues. "The question is: How are we going to move forward together?"

You could have heard a pin drop. Actually, they all did hear a *pen* drop, when Chuck dropped the one he was twirling.

Tigg distributes sheets of paper exactly like the one she received at the conference, with one column titled "existing" and one titled "desired." She asks them all to take their time completing the form and to feel comfortable talking with each other about it.

After a slow start (because the team is still thinking this is some sort of joke), the group starts talking about each of the categories. In fact, they get so engaged in the process, instead of five different forms, they switch to the whiteboard and co-create one form representing all of their ideas. A smiling Tigg watches and deliberately doesn't participate unless the group asks her questions.

Once the group is finished writing, Tigg shares what she had created on her own at the conference. They compare the two documents and, except for some minor word choices (which they determine through dialogue represent the same ideas), the papers are nearly identical.

First, there is a collective sigh of relief. The tension they've been living with for so long is gone, completely gone. Each of them, in their minds, begins forecasting what this change means to their department and to the company... the excitement in the room is tangible. They decide to celebrate with a party!

"Phred you HAVE to bring your world famous carrot cake," says Tigg.

"Of course I will," Phred agrees. "And Chuck, you'll be in charge of the entertainment, as always."

Al asks the group, "Can we play that pin-the-mustache-on-the-man game? It cracks me up when the mustache doesn't even make it on his face."

At the party (and after a few carrot juice cocktails), the staff is feeling relaxed and the conversation shifts to all the positive, unintended consequences the new leadership approach has brought to Carralot. Not only has the management team embraced this process, it has trickled into all parts of the company, driving more openness, trust, and transparency.

"What else can we do to keep this in the forefront?" asks Tigg.

They decide that, as an additional motivator, they will donate a percentage of profits to a foundation they creatively name "Really Carrsalot" for grants and scholarships that are devoted to projects focused on thinking globally about sustainable food production.

Mick, who has been somewhat contemplative and quiet, asks Tigg if C3's management team could all participate in a Human-Assisted Learning experience. He read a fascinating article in the Carrot Topper and has been meaning to ask her about it, except the timing never seemed right. Tigg looks bummed because Mick stole her surprise. She was going to make a big announcement that she's already scheduled a series of initial training for the entire C3 staff (the staff will determine if they want to continue with additional training and of course they will because HAL is so effective). As soon as she catches her initial negative and selfish response of feeling bummed, she reframes her attitude and a broad smile breaks out on her face. *Wow!* She thinks to herself, *isn't it wild that we're all looking to become personally and professionally successful? When you reframe relationships, you create new possibilities!*

The End … or is it just the beginning for your organization?

Appendix

Carralot's situation and transformation is designed to be an entertaining and effective way to introduce people to new possibilities moving your herd, connecting people, and leveraging the strengths of both task-focused and relational leadership. With any luck, you didn't identify too much with the toxic environment in the first part of the story, AND if you did, you're reading this section because you have hope of making positive changes to yourself or your organization. As team Carralot showed, to be wildly successful takes more than simply reading a book, even a book as good as this one. ☺

In our fable, Tigg becomes aware of her role and choices affecting C3 at a conference when she participates in a human-assisted learning experience. As you know, the design of this fable manipulates a role reversal of horses and humans. Therefore, from this point forward, the tools, resources, and information provided will be drawn from evidence and genuine benefits of Equine-Assisted Learning, since human-assisted learning facilitated by animals doesn't really exist (at least not in a formal way).

Tigg's openness to change and personal reflection leads to her "aha" moment, realizing the only thing she could change is herself. She also becomes aware of the unintended negative consequences of her good intentions. Francisco Varela, Chilean biologist, philosopher, and neuroscientist, describes three thresholds of becoming aware: suspension, redirection, and letting go. The process of shifting our attention invites co-creation of an emerging future, taking us from only using information that is historic, based on previous knowledge and existing ways of being, to new, creative, and innovative alternatives.

One trailhead, or beginning, in a successful (hopefully wildly successful) change initiative starts with facilitating a learning environment that supports the outcomes you desire. This simple sentence has a lot of "layers" in it, including understanding human motivation, decision-making, adult learning theory, and I could go on (and on and on). Do not take lightly the importance of effective facilitation. Remember, if you do what you've always done, you will get what you've always gotten. Learning, by its very definition, can be challenging: taking people out of their comfort zones, facing information they may not want to acknowledge, and making choices regarding whether or not that information is useful to help them on their own personal journeys.

Yet, there is a well-known correlation between productivity and participation. Allowing for the self-organization of individuals requires trust and freedom. Providing the "right" amount of trust and freedom begins with leveraging core principles. What is a "core principle?" Through strengthening your core you build a firm foundation, whether you are an individual seeking to improve your leadership, self-awareness, or personal growth or if we are talking about a group of people pursuing team building, improved communication, or conflict resolution. Equine-assisted learning provides wisdom from the natural world about three core principles that best serve us. Simplifying the complexity of change efforts by focusing on our core we can identify keys to unlock the secrets to unimaginable success and joy. Let me briefly explain...

Target your efforts toward the three interconnected guiding principles of the person(s), connection, and movement:

Person(s). People have the power of choice. As we learned in the story during the debriefing of the HAL session, facts are facts; the power of positivity is deciding or choosing what matters and how you want to respond to the facts. People can learn from horses to stay present in the moment, be curious, and intentionally read the environment. Surprisingly, this takes practice for people and is automatic for our four-legged friends. Through people becoming more equine-like, they increase their ability to "be" rather than simply "do". You can create the future you desire by beginning with self-awareness through investing in learning how people (including yourself) are motivated, how different learning and communication styles create confusion and/or clarity, and how our brains are wired.

Connection.   Connection means that we are not alone and improving our self-awareness isn't enough to create the future we desire. While the only person you can change is yourself, an interdependence to others still exists, both those present and not present, that is worthy of attention. Connection is related to energy and how you choose to show up in a relationship to others. Horses respond authentically and non-judgmentally to people in a way that holds them accountable for congruence in their behaviors, thoughts, and beliefs. They "read" people and provide honest feedback. Remember, feedback is always about the sender and may or may not resonate with the receiver, meaning we can decide to take what serves us and let the rest go. Power, position, and hierarchy are also a part of leveraging connections. In equine terms, it is often obvious who is more powerful because the relationship is measured by whichever horse can move the other. Focusing on connection in equine terms leads to improved communication, more genuine relationships, and inviting others to become more authentically present with you.

Movement. As with horses, to control movement of yourself or your organization, you want to control the head. Movement represents life and our basic nature. Equines are prey animals that read the environment in order to survive. Therefore their first reaction to fear is a flight response. Even though humans are by nature predators, when they feel threatened - many humans will physically leave or mentally check out. One of the wonderful lessons equines offer us is that, following a threatening experience, they go back to grazing. They don't keep score, plot revenge, or plan retribution for the next time that a "horse-eating" plastic bag rolls into the pasture. Movement is also about pressure. Pressure is required for the most basic of things, such as breathing; it is pressure that fills and empties our lungs with air. For equines, pressure is a critical learning tool. They move away from it, so when you are getting the behavior you want, you reward them by removing the force. We teach them by making what we want easy and what we don't want difficult, using as little pressure as possible and as much as necessary. By focusing on movement, organizations can develop a culture of trust, failing faster and thus learning from mistakes more quickly which supports innovation and authenticity.

Person, Connection, and Movement are the basis of Kaleidoscope Learning Circle's ("KLC") TriCore Model. KLC's TriCore Model characterizes the foundation of presentations and speaking engagements by Kaleidoscope founder, Dr. Tracy Weber. The Wildly Successful website (www.wildlysuccessfulsolutions.com) will be providing additional resources and program offerings to take your change initiative forward. The website will feature programs, products, and services supporting your efforts to create healthy work environments that embrace customer- and employee-centric cultures that are flexible and adaptable, and develop trust through co-creation. There is also a link to Kaleidoscope Learning Circle's website (www.myklc.com) for those who are interested in a customized equine-assisted learning experience.

Lastly, the following represents a "short list" of the underlying themes, theories, and thought leaders represented in Wildly Successful. I invite you to dig deeper on each of these sites, because you'll find treasures upon treasures of additional resources and information. Happy Trails!

Barry Johnson www.polaritypartnerships.com

Creative Confidence www.creativeconfidence.com

Daniel Pink www.danielpink.com

Freakonomics www.freakonomics.com

Heath Brothers www.heathbrothers.com

Leverage Networks www.leveragenetworks.com

Malcolm Gladwell www.gladwell.com

Margaret Wheatley www.margaretwheatley.com

Marshall Goldsmith www.marshallgoldsmithlibrary.com

Neuroleadership www.neuroleadership.com

Peter Block www.peterblock.com

Presencing Institute www.presencing.com

Project Implicit https://implicit.harvard.edu/implicit/

Shankar Vedantam www.hiddenbrain.org

Society of Organizational Learning www.solonline.org

Systems Thinking in Action www.stiatemenos.com

Ted Talks www.ted.com

Where Do We Go From Here?
Wildly Successful's website, of course!
(www.wildlysuccessfulsolutions.com)

References

Anderson, D, & Anderson L.A. (2013, November 15) How Command and Control as a Change Leadership Style Causes Transformational Change Efforts to Fail. Retrieved from http://changeleadersnetwork.com/free-resources

Arglye, M. (2001). The Psychology of Happiness. East Sussex: Routledge.

Argyris, C., & Schön, D. (1996). Organizational learning II. Reading, MA: Addison-Wesley.

Ariely, D. (2008). Predictably Irrational: The Hidden Forces that Shape Our Decisions. New York, NY: Harper Perennial.

Ariely, D. (2012). The (Honest) Truth About Dishonesty: How We Lie to Everyone – Especially Ourselves. New York, NY: HarperCollins Publishers.

Balasubramanian, V. Organizational Learning and Information Systems. [On-Line] Rutgers University Graduate School of Management. Available: //eies.njit.edu/~333/orglm.html., March 16, 1999.

Bekoff, M (2007). The Emotional Lives of Animals: A leading scientist explores animal joy, sorrow, and empathy- and why they matter. Novato, CA: New World Library.

Belasen, A.T. (2000). Learning the Learning Organization: Communication and Competencies for Managing Change. Albany, NY: State University of New York Press.

Bennett-Goleman, T. (2001). Emotional Alchemy: How the Mind Can Heal the Heart. New York: Harmony Books.

Bennis, W. & Goldsmith, J. (2003). Learning to Lead: A Workbook on Becoming a Leader. New York: Basic Books.

Bennis, W., Spreitzer, G., & Cummings, T. (Eds.). (2001). The Future of Leadership: Today's Top Leadership Thinkers Speak to Tomorrow's Leaders. San Francisco: Jossey-Bass.

Block, P. (1993). Stewardship: Choosing Service Over Self-Interest. San Francisco: Berrett-Koehler.

Block, P. (2003). The Answer to How Is Yes: Acting on What Matters. San Francisco: Berrett-Koehler.

Block, P. (2008). Community: The Structure of Belonging. San Francisco: Berrett-Koehler.

Block, P. (2010). Flawless Consulting: A Guide to Getting Your Expertise Used. San Francisco: Jossey-Bass.

Bohm, D. (1996). On Dialogue. London: Routledge.

Boyatzis, Cowen, Kolb, & Associates. (1995). Innovation in Professional Education. San Francisco: Jossey-Bass.

Broughton, P. (2012). The Art of the Sale: Learning from the Masters About the Business of Life. New York: The Penguin Press.

Burrus, D. (2011). Flash Foresight: How to See the Invisible and Do the Impossible. New York: HarperCollins Publishing.

Camp, J. (2008). The Soul of a Horse: Life lessons from the Herd. New York, NY: Harmony Books.

Childre, D., Martin, H. & Beech, D. (1999). The Heartmath Solution. New York: HarperCollins.

Coens, T. & Jenkins, M. (2002). Abolishing Performance Appraisals: Why They Backfire and What to Do Instead. San Francisco: Berrett-Koehler.

Collins, J. (2001). Good to Great: Why Some Companies Make the Leap...And Others Don't. New York: HarperBusiness.

Coyle, D. (2009). The Talent Code: Greatness Isn't Born. It's Grown. Here's How. New York: Bantam Books.

Csikszentmihalyi, M. (1990). Flow: The Psychology of Optimal Experience. New York: HarperPerennial.

Davis, S. & Meyer, C. (1998). Blur: The Speed of Change in the Connected Economy. New York: Warner Books.

Davis, S., & Meyer, C. (2003). It's Alive: The Coming Convergence of Information, Biology, and Business. New York: Crown Business.

Dewey, J. (1938). Logic: The Theory of Inquiry. New York: Henry Holt.

Diamond, J. (1992). The Third Chimpanzee: The Evolution and Future of the Human Animal. New York: Harper Perennial.

Dionne, E. J. Jr. (Ed.), (1998). Community Works: The Revival of Civil Society in America. Washington, DC: Brookings Institution Press.

Dorrance, B. & Desmond, L (1999). True Horsemanship Through Feel. Guilford, CT: The Lyons Press.

Doyle, T. & Zakrajsek, T. (2011). Learner-Centered Teaching: Putting the Research on Learning Into Practice. Sterling, Virginia: Stylus.

Doyle, T. & Zakrajsek, T. (2013). The New Science of Learning: How to Learn in Harmony with Your Brain. Sterling, Virginia: Stylus.

Duffy, T. M., & Cunningham, D. J. (1996). Constructivism: Implications for the Design and Delivery of Instruction. In D. H. Jonassen (Ed.), Handbooks of Research on Educational Communications and Technology. London: MacMillan.

Edosomwan, J. (1996). Organizational Transformation and Process Reengineering. Delray Beach, Florida: St. Lucie Press.

Fast, J. (2002). Body Language. New York: MJF Books.

Fink, L. (2003). Creating Significant Learning Experiences: An Integrated Approach to Designing College Courses. San Francisco: Jossey-Bass.

Flaherty, J. (1999). Coaching: Evoking Excellence in Others. Boston: Butterworth Heinemann.

Fosnot, C. T. (Ed.). (1996). Constructivism: Theory, Perspective, and Practice. New York: Teachers College Press.

Frank, L. (2001). The Caring Classroom: Using Adventure to Create Community in the Classroom and Beyond. Publisher: Author.

Frank, R. (2007). The Economic Naturalist: In Search of Explanations for Everyday Enigmas. New York: Basic Books.

Fred, T. (2004). Animal Talk: Breaking the codes of animal language. New York, NY: Free Press.

Fritz, R. (1999). The Path of Least Resistance for Managers: Designing Organizations to Succeed. San Francisco: Berrett-Koehler.

Fullan, M. (2000). Change Forces: The Sequel. Philadelphia, Pennsylvania: Falmer Press.

Fullan, M. (2001). Leading in a Culture of Change: Being Effective in Complex Times. San Francisco: Jossey-Bass.

Fulmer, R. & Goldsmith, M. (2001). The Leadership Investment: How the World's Best Organizations Gain Strategic Advantage Through Leadership Development. New York: AMACOM.

Fulmer, R. & Keys, J., (1998). A Conversation with Chris Argyris: The Father of Organizational Learning. Organizational Dynamics, Vol. 27.

Gardner, H. (2004). Changing Minds: The Art and Science of Changing Our Own and Other People's Minds. Boston: Harvard Business School Press.

Gardner, H. (2007). Five Minds for the Future. Boston: Harvard Business School Press.

George, B. (2003). Authentic Leadership: Rediscovering the Secrets to Creating Lasting Value. San Francisco: Jossey-Bass

Gilbert, D. 2005). Stumbling on Happiness. New York: Vintage Books.

Gladwell, M. (2005). Blink: The Power of Thinking without Thinking. New York: Little, Brown, and Company.

Glasser, W. (1998). Choice Theory: A New Psychology of Personal Freedom. New York: HarperPerennial.

Glenn, S. & Nelson, J. (1998). Raising Self-Reliant Children in a Self-Indulgent world: Seven Building blocks for Developing Capable Young People. Rocklin, California: Pima Publishing and Communications.

Goldsmith, M. & Reiter, M. (2009). Mojo: How to Get It, How to Keep It, How to Get It Back, If You Lose It. New York: Hyperion.

Goleman, D. (2000). Working with Emotional Intelligence. New York: Bantam Books.

Goleman, D. (2006). Social Intelligence: The New Science of Human Relationships. New York: Bantam Books.

Goleman, D. (2009). Ecological Intelligence: How Knowing the Hidden Impacts of What We Buy Can Change Everything. New York: Broadway Books.

Goleman, D. (2011). Leadership: The Power of Emotional Intelligence Selected Writings. Publisher: Author.

Goleman, D., Boyatzis, R., & McKee, A. (2002). Primal Leadership: Realizing the Power of Emotional Intelligence. Boston: Harvard Business School Press.

Gosling, S. (2008). Snoops: What Stuff Says about You. New York: Basic Books.

Grandin, T. & Johnson, C (2005). Animals in Translation: Using the mysteries of autism to decode animal behavior. New York, NY: Scribner.

Gunter, J. (2007). Teaching Horse: Rediscovering leadership. Bloomington, IN: AuthorHouse.

Hallberg, L. (2008). Walking the Way of the Horse: Exploring the power of the horse-human relationship. Bloomington, IN: iUniverse.

Hall, E. T. (1989). Beyond Culture. New York: Anchor Books/Doubleday.

Heath, C. & Heath, D. (2013). Decisive: How to Make Better Choices in Life and Work. New York: Random House.

Heath, C. & Heath, D. (2007). Made to Stick: Why Some Ideas Survive and Others Die. New York: Crown Business.

Heath, C. & Heath, D. (2010). Switch: How to Change Things When Change Is Hard. New York: Crown Business.

Heskett, J., Sasser, W. & Schlesiger, L. (1997). The Service Profit Chain: How Leading Companies Link Profit and Growth to Loyalty, Satisfaction, and Value. New York: The Free Press.

Hesselbein, F. (1998a). Journey to Transformation. Leader to Leader.

Hesselbein, F., Goldsmith, M., & Beckhard, R. (Eds.). (1996). The Leader of the Future. New York: The Drucker Foundation.

Hogan, L., Metzger, D., & Peterson, B. Intimate Nature: The Bond Between Women & Animals. New York: Fawcett Books.

Huba, E. M., & Freed, J. E. (2000). Learner-Centered Assessment on College Campuses: Shifting the Focus from Teaching to Learning. Boston: Allyn & Bacon.

Hunt, R. (1978). Horse Sense For People. Wipperfuerth, Germany: Ute Kierdorf Verlag.

Hutchens, D. (1999). Shadows of the Neanderthal: Illuminating the Beliefs that Limit Our Organizations. Pegasus Communications, Inc.

Hutchens, D. (2000). Outlearning the Wolves: Surviving and Thriving in a Learning Organization. Pegasus Communications, Inc.

Hutchens, D. (2000). The Lemming Dilemma: Living with Purpose, Leading with Vision. Pegasus Communications, Inc.

Hutchens, D. (2005). Listening to the Volcano: Conversations That Open Our Minds to New Possibilities. Pegasus Communications, Inc.

Irwin, C. & Weber, C (1998). Horses Don't Lie: What horses teach us about our natural capacity for awareness, confidence, courage, and trust. New York, NY: Marlowe & Company.

Isaacs, W. (1999). Dialogue and the Art of Thinking Together: A Pioneering Approach to Communicating in Business and in Life. New York: Currency.

James, M. & Jongeward, D. (1971). Born to Win: Transactional Analysis with Gestalt Experiments. Philippines: Addison-Wesley Publishing Company, Inc.

Jaworski, J. (1998). Synchronicity: The Inner Path of Leadership. San Francisco: Berrett-Koehler.

Jaworski, J. (2012). Source: The Inner Path of Knowledge Creation. San Francisco: Berrett-Koehler.

Johnson, B. (1996). Polarity Management: Identifying and Managing Unsolvable Problems. Amherst, Massachusetts: HRD Press, Inc.

Joiner, B. L. (1994). Fourth Generation Management: The New Business Consciousness. New York: McGraw-Hill.

Jung, C.G. (1969). Synchronicity: An Acausal Connecting Principle. Princeton University Press.

Kahler, T. (2006). The Mystery Management or How to Solve the Mystery of Mismanagement. Little Rock, Arkansas: Kahler Communications, Inc.

Karpman, S. (1968). Fairy Tales & Script Drama Analysis. Transactional Analysis Bulletin. Vol. 7, No. 26.

Katzenbach, J. & Smith D. (1993). The Wisdom of Teams: Creating the High Performance Organization. Harvard Business School Press.

Kelley, T. & Kelley, D. (2013). Creative Confidence: Unleashing the Creative Potential Within Us All. New York: Crown Business.

Kim, W. & Mauborgne, R. (2005). Blue Ocean Strategy: How to Create Uncontested Market Space and Make the Competition Irrelevant. Boston: Harvard Business School Press.

Klein, S. (2002). The Science of Happiness: How Our Brains Make Us Happy – and What We Can Do to Get Happier. New York: Marlowe & Company.

Kline, P. & Saunders, B. (1998). Ten Steps to a Learning Organization. Arlington, Virginia: Great Ocean Publishers.

Knapp, S. (2013). More Than a Mirror: Horses, Humans, & Therapeutic Practices. Publisher: Author.

Knowles, M., H., E. & Swanson, R. (1998). The Adult Learner: The Definitive Classic in Adult Education and Human Resource Development. Houston: Gulf Publishing Company.

Koenig, B. (2013, February 28). We Need the Capacity of a Collective Play with Complexity. Retrieved on February 28, 2013 from www.bgi.edu/changing-business/we-need-the-capacity-of-a-collective-to-play-with-complexity/.

Koestenbaum, P., & Block, P. (2001). Freedom and Accountability at Work: Philosophic Insight to the Real World. San Francisco: Jossey-Bass/Pfeiffer.

Kohn, Alfie. (1990). The Brighter Side of Human Nature: Altruism & Empathy in Everyday Life. BasicBooks.

Kolb, D. (1984) Retrieved on December 10, 2013. http://academic.regis.edu/ed205.

Lanning, M. (1998). Delivering Profitable Value. New York: Perseus Books.

Lencioni, P. (2002). Getting Naked: The Five Dysfunctions of a Team: A Leadership Fable. San Francisco: Jossey-Bass/Pfeiffer.

Lencioni, P. (2010). Getting Naked: A Business Fable...about shedding the three fears that sabotage client loyalty. San Francisco: Jossey-Bass/Pfeiffer.

Levitt, D. & Dubner, D. (2014). Think Like A Freak. New York: HarperCollins Publishers.

Linkner, J. (2011). Disciplined Dreaming: A Proven System to Drive Breakthrough Creativity. San Francisco: Jossey-Bass/Pfeiffer.

Lipman-Blumen, J. (1996). Connective Leadership: Managing in a Changing World. Oxford: University Press.

Loeb, P. (1999). Soul of a Citizen: Living with Conviction in a Cynical Time. New York: St. Martin's Griffin.

May, M. (2009). In Pursuit of Elegance: Why the Best Ideas Have Something Missing. New York: Broadway Books.

May, R. (1975). The Courage to Create. New York: W.W. Norton & Company, Inc.

Merriam, S. & Caffarella, R. (1999). Learning in Adulthood: A Comprehensive Guide. San Francisco: Jossey-Bass.

Miller, R. M. (1999). Understanding the Ancient Secrets of the Horse's Mind. Neenah, WI: The Russell Meerdink Company, Ltd.

Miller, R. M. & Lamb, Rick (2005). The Revolution in Horsemanship and What it Means to Mankind. Guilford, CT: The Lyons Press.

Miller, R. M. (2007). Natural Horsemanship Explained: From heart to hands. Guilford, CT:The Lyons Press.

Miller, W. & C'deBaca, J. (2001). Quantum Change: When Epiphanies and Sudden Insights Transform Ordinary Lives. New York: The Guilford Press.

Morgan, G. (1997). Images of Organization. (2nd. edition). Sage Publications.

Naisbitt, J. & Aburdene, P. (1985). Re-Inventing the Corporation: Transforming Your Job and Your Company for the Information Society. New York: Warner Books.

National Research Council. (2000). How People Learn: Brain, Mind, Experience, and School. Washington D.C.: National Academy Press.

Niven, D. (2000). The 100 Simple Secrets of Happy People: What Scientists Have Learned and How You Can Use it. New York: HarperSanFrancisco.

Pandya, M. & Shell, R. (2005). Lasting Leadership: What You Can Learn From the Top 25 Business People of Our Times. Wharton School Publishing.

Patwell, B. & Seashore, E. (2006). Triple Impact Coaching: Use-of-Self in the Coaching Process. Maryland: Bingham House Books.

Pert, C. (1997). Molecules of Emotion: The Science Behind Mind-Body Medicine. New York: A Touchstone Book.

Peters, T. (1998). The Circle of Innovation: You Can't Shrink Your Way to Greatness. New York: Alred A. Knopf.

Pine, B. & Gilmore, J. (1999). The Experience Economy: Work Is Theatre & Every Business a Stage. Publisher: Author.

Pink, D. (2006). A Whole New Mind: Why Right-Brainers Will Rule the Future. New York: Riverhead Books.

Pink, D. (2009). Drive: The Surprising Truth about What Motivates Us. New York: Riverhead Books.

Pink, D. (2012). To Sell is Human: The Surprising Truth about Moving Others. New York: RiverheadBooks.

Pollard, W., (1998). Education and the Workforce. Testimony to the Education and The Workforce Committee of the House of Representatives, Washington, DC.

Prahalad, C.K. & Ramaswamy, V. (2004). The Future of Competition: Co-Creating Unique Value with Customers. Boston: Harvard Business School Press.

Radin, D. (2006). Entangled Minds: Extrasensory Experiences in a Quantum Reality. New York: Pocket Books.

Rashid, M. (2005). Horsemanship Through Life. Boulder, CO: Johnson Books.

Ray, P. & Anderson, S. (2000). The Cultural Creatives: How 50 Million People Are Changing the World. New York: Harmony Books.

Regier, N. & King, J. (2013). Beyond Drama: Transcending Energy Vampires. Newton, Kansas: Next Element Publishing.

Ridley, M. (1996). The Origins of Virtue: Human Instincts and the Evolution of Cooperation. New York: Penguin Books.

Roberts, M. (1996) The Man Who Listens to Horses. New York: Random House.

Roberts, M. (2000). Horse Sense For People. New York, NY: Penguin Putnam Inc.

Robinson, G. & Rose, M. (2004). A Leadership Paradox: Influencing Others by Defining Yourself. Bloomington, Indiana: AuthorHouse.

Rock, D. (2009). Your Brain at Work: Strategies for Overcoming Distraction, Regaining Focus, and Working Smarter All Day Long. New York: HarperCollins Books.

Ross, Sherwood, & Reuter (1997). Envisioning Goals Key for Progress in Working World Management Expert Says Workers Need to Visualize Future to Achieve Success and Further Their Careers. Rocky Mountain News.

Satori, J. (1999). Synchronicity: The Entrepreneur's Edge. Boston: Butterworth Heinemann.

Scanlan, L. (1998). Wild about Horses. New York: HarperCollins.

Scharmer, O. (2007). Theory U: Leading from the Future as It Emerges. Massachusetts: Society of Organizational Learning.

Scharmer, O. & Kaufer, K. (2013). Leading from the Emerging Future. San Francisco: Berrett-Koehler Publishers, Inc.

Schneider, B., Gunnarson, S., Niles-Jolly, K. (1994). Creating the Climate and Culture of Success. Organizational Dynamics, Vol. 23.

Scholtes, P., Joiner, B., & Streibel, B., (1996). The Team Handbook (2nd ed.). Wisconsin: Oriel Incorporated.

Schwartz, P. (1996). The Art of the Long View: Planning for the Future in an Uncertain World. New York: Currency Doubleday.

Schwartz, P., Leyden, P. & Hyatt, J. (1999). The Long Boom: A Vision for the Coming Age of Prosperity. Reading Massachusetts: Perseus Books.

Schwarz, R. (2002). The Skilled Facilitator: A Comprehensive Resource for Consultants, Facilitators, Managers, Trainers, and Coaches. San Francisco: Jossey-Bass.

Senge, P., Kleiner, A., Roberts, C., Ross, R., & Smith, B. (1994). The Fifth Discipline Fieldbook: Strategies and Tools for Building a Learning Organization. New York: Currency Doubleday.

Senge, P., Kleiner, A., Roberts, C., Ross, R., Roth, G. & Smith, B. (1999). The Dance of Change: The Challenges to Sustaining Momentum in Learning Organizations. New York: Currency Doubleday.

Senge, P. & Kofman, F., (1993). Communities of Commitment: The Heart of Learning Organizations. Organizational Dynamics. Special Issue on the Learning Organization.

Senge, P., Schwarmer, C., Jaworski, J. & Flowers, B. (2004). Presence: An Exploration of Profound Change in People, Organizations, and Society. New York: CurrencyDoubleday.

Senge, P., Smith, B., Kruschwitz, N., Laur, J., & Schley, S. (2008). The Necessary Revolution: How Individuals and Organizations Are Working Together to Create a Sustainable World. New York: Doubleday.

Senge, Peter, M. (1996). Rethinking Leadership in the Learning Organization. The Systems Thinker.

Shor, I. (1992). Empowering Education: Critical Teaching for Social Change. Chicago: University of Chicago Press.

Siegel, B. (1990). Peace, Love & Healing: Bodymind Communication & the Path to Self-Healing an Exploration. New York: Perennial Library.

Smith, J. K. (1990). Alternative Research Paradigms and the Problem of Criteria. In E. Guba (ELI), The Paradigm Dialog. Thousand Oaks, CA: Sage.

Spears, L. (Eds.). (1995). Reflections on Leadership: How Robert K. Greenleaf's Theory of Servant-Leadership Influenced Today's Top Management Thinkers. New York: John Wiley & Sons, Inc.

Spears, L. & Lawrence, M. (Eds.). (2002). Focus on Leadership: Servant-Leadership for the 21st Century. New York: John Wiley & Sons, Inc.

Sterman, J. (2000). Business Dynamics: Systems Thinking and Modeling for a Complex World. McGraw-Hill Higher Education.

Sugarman, D., Doherty, K., Garvey, D. & Gass, M. (2000). Reflective Learning: Theory and Practice. Dubuque, Iowa: Kendall/Hunt Publishing Company.

Swain, S. (1998). Studying Teachers' Transformations: Reflection as Methodology, (Participants in the Writing Opens New Dimensions of Educational Realms) (Reflective Classroom Culture as a Part of the Portfolio Process). Mississippi State University, Mississippi Writing/Thinking Institute.

Sweeney, L. & Meadows, D. (1995). The Systems Thinking Playbook: Exercises to Stretch and Build Learning and Systems Thinking Capabilities. Publisher: Author.

Taleb, N. (2007). The Black Swan: The Impact of the Highly Improbable. New York: Random House.

Taylor, W. & LaBarre, P. (2006). Mavericks at Work: Why the Most Original Minds in Business Win. New York: HarperCollins

Tellington-Jones, L. & Taylor, S (1995). Getting in Touch with Horses: How to assess and influence personality, potential, and performance. Wykey, Shrewsbury: Kenilworth Press.

Thayler, R. & Sunstein, C. (2008). Nudge: Improving Decisions about Health, Wealth, and Happiness. New Haven & London: Yale University Press.

Tice, L. (2005). Smart Talk for Achieving Your Potential: 5 Steps to Get You from Here to There. Seattle: Pacific Institute Publishing.

Trout, J. (1999). The Power of Simplicity: A Management Guide to Cutting Through the Nonsense and Doing Things Right. New York: McGraw-Hill.

Tucker, J. A. & Tucker P. M. (2012). We are higher education, and we change not. In Pawluk S. & Bietz, G. (Eds) Seventh-day Adventist Higher Education in North America: Theological Perspectives & Current Issues. Nampa, ID: Pacific Press Publishing Association.

Tugend, A. (2011). Better by Mistake: The Unexpected Benefits of Being Wrong. New York: Riverhead Books.

Van de Ven, A. H., & Poole, M. S. (1995). Explaining Development and Change in Organizations. Academy of Management Review.

Vedantam, S. (2010). The Hidden Brain: How Our Unconscious Minds Elect Presidents, Control Markets, Wage Wars and Save Our Lives. New York: Spiegel & Grau.

Vella, J. (2002). Learning to Listen. Learning to Teach. The Power of Dialogue in Educating Adults. San Francisco: Jossey-Bass.

Warren, K., Sakofs, M., & Hunt, J. (Eds.). (1995). The Theory of Experiential Education: A Collection of Articles Addressing the Historical, Philosophical, Social, and Psychological Foundations of Experiential Education. Dubuque, Iowa: Kendall/Hunt Publishing Company.

Weber, T. (1999). Researching Potential Partners for an Equestrian Learning Center in Frankenmuth, MI. Master's Thesis. Rochester Institute of Technology. Rochester, New York.

Weber, T. (2002). The Design, Implementation, and Assessment of Initial Change and Growth in a Local Voluntary Organization and Its Members. Doctoral Dissertation. Andrews University. Berrien Springs, Michigan.

Wheatley, M. (1997, July). Command and Control. Leader to Leader.

Wheatley, M. (1999). Leadership and the New Science: Discovering Order in a Chaotic World. San Francisco Berrett-Koehler Publishers, Inc.

Wheatley, M. (2005). Finding Our Way: Leadership for an Uncertain Time. San Francisco Berrett-Koehler Publishers, Inc.

Zigarmi, D., Blanchard, K., O'Conner, M., & Edeburn, C. (2005). The Leader Within: Learning Enough about Yourself to Lead Others. Upper Saddle River, New Jersey: Prentice Hall.

Zohar, D. & Marshall, I. (2000). SQ: Connecting with Our Spiritual Intelligence. Publisher: Author.

About the Author

<u>Wildly Successful</u> author, Dr. Tracy Weber, founded Kaleidoscope Learning Circle near Frankenmuth, Michigan to facilitate building healthy relationships and creating new possibilities through partnering with horses. Her learner-centered and competency-based graduate work laid the foundation for KLC's customized program designs. Kaleidoscope combines Tracy's passion for horses with her desire to help people find their authentic self, believing that profound change begins with personal transformation. As an entrepreneur, farm owner, and pioneer in the field of Equine-Assisted Learning (EAL), her network of professionals and friends in the equine-assisted industry is far-reaching across disciplines and geography. KLC's clients range from financial institutions, nonprofit organizations, small businesses, departments of larger companies, and college students. A more complete list and links to corresponding photos can be found on the Kaleidoscope website (<u>www.myklc.com</u>).

In addition to delivering professional development and personal growth programs, Tracy is on faculty at Rochester Institute of Technology (RIT), Prescott College, Michigan State University (MSU), and Northwood University. As part of her courses in Leadership and Customer Relationship Management, she has incorporated equine-assisted learning as far away as Dubai and Croatia. She has presented at a variety of conferences including the Lilly Conference on Higher Education and Learning, PATH International, and the Association of Experiential Educators to name a few. Tracy is the 2011 PATH International Membership National Leadership Award recipient and she was named Swan Valley High School's Distinguished Alumni that same year. Also, in 2010, she received the Catalyst Award from the Michigan Horse Council. More recently, Tracy received the

2014 Great Lakes Bay Region YWCA Entrepreneur Award and was the 2014 recipient of the Dr. Richard Marecki Memorial Award

Tracy is an active community member and currently serves on the Executive Board of Saginaw County Business and Education Partnership. A graduate of the Great Lakes Bay Regional Leadership Institute, she is a member of the Frankenmuth Noon Rotary, Saginaw County, Frankenmuth, and Birch Run Chambers of Commerce, Inforum, and is involved with several international trade associations.

Before founding Kaleidoscope Learning Circle, llc., Tracy's career included experience in marketing and leadership positions in for-profit, nonprofit, and governmental sectors. Her areas of expertise include organizational behavior and change, personal growth and professional development, developing competency based initiatives, women's issues, and an emphasis on understanding systems, group dynamics, and leadership. She is a graduate of Swan Valley High School, earned a Bachelor's Degree in Advertising from MSU, a Master's in Service Management from RIT, and earned a Ph.D. in Leadership from Andrews University. Tracy is a devoted parent of two daughters, Kaitlyn and Carlye, who are both in college, an active volunteer, and a life-long horse lover. Her financé, Randy Bierlein, lives in Frankenmuth. Complete resume at www.myklc.com.

CPSIA information can be obtained at www.ICGtesting.com
Printed in the USA
BVOW11s1449240315

392970BV00002B/3/P